THE DEDICATED LIFE

A Study on the Forgotten Topic of Holiness

Paul M Hanssen

SEVEN PILLARS CHURCH COMMUNICATIONS

Apostle Paul and Sis Gwen Hanssen
Founders of Seven Pillars Church of Praise Int'l

TABLE OF CONTENTS   PAGE

INTRODUCTION

Holiness is one of the most misunderstood and therefore, possibly one of the most avoided subjects in the church world today. I have often referred to holiness as the forgotten topic within the modern church.

Holiness is viewed by many simply as a list of rules of *do's and don'ts*. In an attempt to produce a holy flock, many church leaders throughout New Testament history have taught their followers to observe a certain pattern of behavior, display a particular appearance, adhere to a list of daily obligations, and follow a set of religious duties. Many believe that holiness can only be acquired by following a strict regiment of religious rules.

Even though God does require obedience from His people, and even though His Word offers many commands for His Church to follow, the observing of the commandments alone do not make a person holy. For example, keeping the Sabbath day and attending *church* on either Saturday or Sunday does not make anyone holy. Even though the observing of the Sabbath is practiced in obedience to God's commandment, the observance alone does not hallow the observer. A believer can obey a whole list of commandments and still not be holy.

Many religious observances are both morally good and physically healthy. However, fulfilling these deeds alone does not produce that for which they are observed. Holiness is not obtained simply by doing that which is good. Multitudes of people do good deeds every day of their lives. However, they are not made holy due to their deeds.

God requires that His people be holy. Actually, God not only requires this, He demands it. Yet, the very thing that God demands can be implemented and performed in such a way that causes disgust in the eyes of God. It is possible to do a right thing, a good thing, in the wrong way.

He that killeth an ox is as if he slew a man; he that sacrificeth a lamb, as if he cut off a dog's neck; he that offereth an oblation, as if he offered swine's blood; he that burneth incense, as if he blessed an idol. Yea, they have chosen their own ways, and their soul delighteth in their abominations. (Isaiah 66:3)

This verse causes my attention to spike. According to the Law of Moses, God, Himself, required the ox as a whole burnt offering. God also required the lamb as a sin offering. It was God who gave the laws concerning the offering of the holy oblations. God was the one who ordered the offering of the incense. However, in the days of Isaiah, why was God so turned off by the observance of that which He, Himself, had required?

The LORD viewed the sacrifice of the whole burnt offering as if a man had been slain. What? Seriously? How many people in Isaiah's day offered an ox upon the altar only for God to respond by saying, "In my eyes you just killed a man?"

In those days, the LORD also viewed the sacrifice of the sin offering lamb as if a dog's neck had been sliced. This is totally repugnant and disgusting, yet how many offered their lamb whilst assuming that God's will was being accomplished?

The LORD also likened the offering of the freewill oblations to that of offering swine's blood upon His holy altar. Can this get any worse?

The LORD hated the stench of the incense that the priests burned upon the Golden Altar in the Holy Place. He likened the incense offering to that of blessing idols. On the other hand, when the incense was offered in the manner in which God required, He delighted in the fragrance of the incense and accepted it as a sweet smelling savor.

These questions therefore remain, "How is it possible that something that God required and delighted in became so distained and disgusting in His eyes? How could a right thing be executed in a wrong way? What turned God off?" We find the answer to these questions in Isaiah, chapter sixty-six.

...but to this man will I look, even to him that is poor and of a contrite spirit, and trembleth at my word. (Isaiah 66:2b)

Yea, they have chosen their own ways, and their soul delighteth in their abominations. (Isaiah 66:3b)

First of all, it was not the offering of the sacrifices to which God sought in seeking for that which delighted His heart. If this were the case, He would have been thrilled with the ox, the lamb, the freewill oblations, and the incense. Instead, He was looking for something else. What was He looking for?

Obviously, the blood of the sacrifices and the fragrant incense that was released in the Holy Place, along with the freewill oblations offered unto God, did not move God's heart. God was looking beyond that which was placed upon the altar. More than anything, God was looking at the condition and the position of the spirit. It is the position of the heart and spirit that is the key to what makes the difference. It is the condition of the spirit that causes God to either accept or reject a sacrifice! It is the condition of the heart that causes God to smile or to frown upon acts of obedience.

The sacrifices that were offered upon the altar were to reflect the attitude, brokenness, contrition, repentance, and humility of the heart and spirit of the ones who were offering the sacrifice. God always looks beyond the outward appearance. God always looks into the heart (1 Samuel 16:7). Our outward actions stem from our inner being. Whether or not the obedience and the sacrifices of our life produce that which God demands, depends on the position of the heart. The visible deeds that are performed by the believer may appear to be right and may even be in accordance to that which God's will demands. However, if the heart is wrong, then the deed is also wrong. If the heart is not toward God, then neither is the sacrifice!

In such cases, God says, "You have chosen your own way and your soul delights in your own abominations." (Isaiah 66:2b). These are harsh words. Doing a right thing in our own way is not acceptable to God, and neither are the outward sacrifices accepted when the soul is taking pleasure in personal abominations.

Taking pleasure in abominations simply means to delight in idolatrous practices. An abomination means something that is disgusting and idolatrous. Idols of any form have always been considered an abomination to God. (Deuteronomy 29:17, 2 Kings 21:11, Ezekiel 6:9).

Many of the religious practices that are performed by *church people* have become a form of idolatry.

Christians of all manner of persuasions take pleasure in idolatrous practices that are an abomination to God. Most of these people are totally oblivious to the idols they serve. The reason that many are unconscious of the disgusting practice of idolatry is because some of the practices that are performed are acts of obedience to God's Word; at least that's what they believe. Yet, these same practices are a stench in God's nostrils because a right thing is being performed in the wrong way.

Holiness is not obtained by outward deeds and actions unless the heart is involved. In this book, we will see what holiness is and how it can become a reality in the life of a sincere saint of God. True holiness can only be obtained through the dedication of the heart. No amount of personal sacrifice can make a person holy. Only a dedicated life unto God can obtain and exhibit true holiness!

CHAPTER

Chapter One

BE YE HOLY

For it is written, Be ye holy; for I am holy.
1 Peter 1:16

The word for holiness in Hebrew is *kaw-doshe* קָדוֹשׁ, from the root word *kaw-dash* קָדַשׁ. The words *kaw-doshe/kaw-dash* mean: sacred (ceremonially or morally), to be pronounced clean, sanctuary, consecrated, set apart, dedicated, hallowed, be prepared, keep, proclaim, purified, and sanctified one.

The power of holiness is not obtained by that which a person *'does'*. Rather, the power of holiness is manifest by that which a person *'is'*. Holiness is not observed in *doing*, but rather in *being*.

In 1 Peter 1:16, God commanded His people to *BE* holy; He did not command that His people *DO* holy. Holiness is therefore a state of being, rather than the performing of a list of activities. However, the fruit and the result of *being* will always lead to *doing*.

The focus of true holiness is about *being* consecrated, dedicated, set apart, devoted and hallowed *unto God*. One cannot *do* separation unto God. We can be only *be* separated unto God. We can do something in one moment, but then in the next moment we can be doing something else. However, when something 'is', it remains 'as is'. For example, an apple tree always produces apples because it *is* an apple tree. It does not produce apples one moment and then oranges the next. In like manner, our lives will produce the fruit of who we *are*, and not of what we *do*. What we do should be the fruit or the product of who we are. Jesus said, "By their fruits ye shall know them." (Matthew 7:20).

God commands us to <u>be holy</u> as <u>He is holy</u>. How can God possibly ask such a tall order of us who are born in sin? How can God possibly require from a fallen creature the same kind of holiness that He, Himself, is adorned with? How can sinful man possibly master holiness in the likeness of God's holiness? This seems totally impossible, and most definitely humanly impossible. Does it not?

There is no holiness so pure, clean, sincere, full of love and as genuine as the holiness of God. The very essence of God's nature, person and presence is holy. He is in every aspect holy!

- God does not need to separate Himself from sin to be holy, since He knows no sin.
- God has no flesh to deny Himself for the sake of becoming holy.
- God does not need to adorn Himself in certain attire to be holy.
- God does not need to observe certain rules or perform particular ceremonies in order to proclaim His holiness.
- God does not have to live up to a particular standard to manifest holiness.

Rather, God is who He is because He is God:

- God *is* holy. He *is* dedicated, consecrated and set apart to *be* who He *is*!
- God is dedicated to His own Name, Will, Plan and Purpose.
- God is holy because of who He is, not because of what He does!

God is set apart from all others. He is Holy, Holy, Holy, in all aspects of His triune being. There is no part of God that is not entirely and absolutely hallowed consecrated. He is completely and utterly dedicated to His own will and purpose. Holiness is the very essence of who God is. As a matter of fact, His very name is Holy!

For he that is mighty hath done to me great things; and holy is his name. (Luke 1:49)

And one cried unto another, and said, Holy, holy, holy, is the LORD of hosts: the whole earth is full of his glory. (Isaiah 6:3)

Holiness is the state of *being* consecrated, set apart, dedicated, and hallowed *unto something*, or *someone*. The Word of God is very clear concerning the manner in which He desires for His people to be holy.

*And ye shall be **holy unto me**: for I the LORD am holy, and have **severed you** from other people, that ye should be mine. (Leviticus 20:26)* (Highlights added by the author)

Holiness is being set apart, or dedicated **unto** God. Holiness is about being dedicated to God's person, dedicated to His will, and set apart for His purpose and plan. Holiness is about being hallowed unto His Name and living a life that is consecrated and dedicated unto Him who purchased you.

The command to *be holy as He is holy* is God desiring for mankind to dedicate himself unto Him, just as He is dedicated unto His own purpose. God has severed us from all people to be His own. Hence, He requires that His purchased possession be holy, devoted, dedicated and set apart unto Him!

God *severs* His people unto Himself. The word severed in Hebrew is the word *taw-dal* which means to divide, separate, distinguish, differ, select, put a difference between, and make separate.

It has always been, and still remains God's purpose, for His people to be set apart and distinguished from the world. This distinction should be visible in the believer's mannerisms, actions, behavior, reactions, presentation, dress, and verbal communication. In other words, this distinction should be visible in every aspect of a believer's life.

Living a dedicated life unto God is not accomplished by adhering to a list of religious rules. Dedication begins in the heart. If the heart is not dedicated unto God first and foremost, then neither is the life that you live.

Dedication is the act of being committed unto something, or someone. Dedication is to be devoted to something, or someone. Dedication is to have single-minded loyalty. Dedication is to be set apart unto God's intended purpose and reason for which we exist.

When dedication is made unto God from the heart, nothing that He requires of us is too great or too small. No sacrifice that He may demand is too much to offer. No deed is too great to perform. No command is too heavy to obey. The individual who possesses a dedicated heart will live a life that reflects their dedication. The reason that the Church today is so full of uncommitted, unclean, disloyal, and double minded people is because the doctrine of dedication unto God has become a forgotten subject.

CHAPTER

Chapter Two

THE TEMPLE OF GOD

Holiness is a fundamental principle that God calls His people to live by. Some believe that holiness is only to be expected and displayed in the lives of the *spiritually mature*. Many are of the opinion that only those who are spiritually *of age* need to consider holiness and that the mention of holiness does not apply to those who are younger in the Faith. This is not true! Holiness and sanctification begin to work in us the moment that we accept Jesus' work of salvation.

But we are bound to give thanks alway to God for you, brethren beloved of the Lord, because God hath from the beginning chosen you to salvation through sanctification of the Spirit and belief of the truth: (1 Thessalonians 2:13).

The word sanctification means: purification, the state of purity, holiness, make holy, consecration, hallow, be holy, sacred, and to be blameless.

From the very beginning of time, and moreover from the moment that we accepted Jesus as our

Savior, God has purposed for His people to walk and to live in sanctification and holiness. To be saved means to be purchased. The redeemed are purchased by the blood of Jesus. The redeemed are the possession of the One who has purchased them.

Take heed therefore unto yourselves, and to all the flock, over the which the Holy Ghost hath made you overseers, to feed the church of God, which he hath purchased with his own blood. (Acts 20:28)

When a purchase is made, it is done with a specific purpose in mind. For example, when someone purchases shampoo, I doubt they would use the shampoo to wash their dishes. Shampoo is produced and sold with a specific purpose in mind. The purpose of shampoo is to wash the hair. Nobody uses shampoo to wash a car or to scrub the floors. Shampoo is designed and *dedicated*, as it were, for a particular use and purpose.

I recall some years ago a particular day in which I needed to do some laundry. As usual, I was in a hurry. Not taking the time to read the labels on the bottles that were arrayed in order on a shelf above my washing machine, I grabbed a plastic container assuming that it was laundry detergent. I proceeded to pour its content into the washing machine. Upon completion of the washing cycle, I discovered that it wasn't laundry detergent! It was floor cleaner. Needless to say, all of the clothes were ruined. I had used a liquid that was dedicated and purposed for cleaning floors, but definitely not for cleaning clothes.

In like manner, God designed and created us for a *dedicated purpose*. Mankind, however, has walked away from God's purpose. But through Jesus, and His work on Calvary's cross, the rogue creation has been purchased by the Redeemer and has been granted the opportunity to become rededicated to God's original purpose and plan.

To reiterate once again, true holiness is dedication unto purpose: God is the purpose! God is the purpose and the reason for living! All creation exists by Him and for Him.

For by him were all things created, that are in heaven, and that are in earth, visible and invisible, whether they be thrones, or dominions, or principalities, or powers: all things were created by him, and for him: (Colossians 1:16)

I said all of that to say that the process of sanctification and holiness begins the moment the purchase is made. The moment that a person accepts Jesus as their Savior, the journey of sanctification and holiness begins.

What? know ye not that your body is the temple of the Holy Ghost which is in you, which ye have of God, and ye are not your own? For ye are bought with a price: therefore glorify God in your body, and in your spirit, which are God's (1 Corinthians 6:19-20).

The child of God has been purchased at a very dear price. You and I are not our own. In other words, a believer should no longer live life to or for *self*. The life of a born-again believer should not be dedicated to the wishes, wants, ways, thoughts, ideas, plans or purpose of self. Once you are purchased, your life becomes destined for the purpose for which you exist.

Holiness is therefore living life unto the purpose for which you are dedicated. Holiness is living unto God who made you for Himself. The work and the manifestation of holiness began the day that you accepted God's work of redemption. The work of sanctification continues to grow and expand throughout the life of a dedicated vessel. As you draw closer and nearer to God, His sanctifying work increases and intensifies.

The Apostle Paul told the Corinthians that they were bought with a price. Therefore, they were to glorify God in their bodies and in their spirits because they belonged to God. This is dedication; this is holiness!

God purposed a sanctuary to be built.

And let them make me a sanctuary; that I may dwell among them. According to all that I shew thee, after the pattern of the tabernacle, and the pattern of all the instruments thereof, even so shall ye make it (Exodus 25:8-9).

The word *sanctuary* comes from the Hebrew root word Kaw-dash which means holiness, dedicated, and consecrated. The sanctuary, namely the Tabernacle of Moses and subsequently the Tabernacle of David and the Temple of Solomon, were structures that were dedicated and set apart for a particular purpose. These structures were to host God's residing glory and presence and were to be used as temples where God was honored and worshipped. These places were revered and respected because of the purpose unto which they were set apart and dedicated. They were holy places.

The Old Testament tabernacles and temples give the believer a graphic picture and a prophetic foreshadow of the living temple that God has called and purposed for His people to be as His purchased possession.

Many have argued that *holiness* is an Old Testament doctrine. Therefore, under the New Testament Order of Grace they believe that there is no need to discuss or to focus on this matter. However, that could not be further from the Truth!

Know ye not that ye are the temple of God, and that the Spirit of God dwelleth in you? If any man defile the temple of God, him shall God destroy; for the temple of God is holy, which temple ye are (1 Corinthians 3:16-17)

Paul made it very clear to the Corinthians that as God's possession in the New Testament era they were the living temple and sanctuary of God. The requirements that God gave concerning His temple are the same today as they were yesterday. He still demands that His temple be holy, dedicated, and set apart unto the purpose for which the temple is erected.

The purpose of the temple is to be the dwelling place of God's Spirit: the dwelling of His divine holy presence and glory. The temple is God's residence. It is to be a place where His throne and kingdom are established. The purchased people of God are purposed as a sanctuary for Him in the earth among men; a place from which His glory and presence are made manifest.

God has always required that His residence be clean, sanctified, and holy. The laws for a functioning temple that hosts God's presence remain the same today as they did yesterday. (We will look more into this subject in the following chapter).

The question that we should be asking ourselves concerning holiness is not, *'What should I do?'*, but rather *'what should I be'*? What is my purpose? What is the purpose of the temple of God? Once I understand what my purpose is and what God requires of me as a dedicated vessel, then I can then begin to *do* that for which I have been set apart. *Doing* must have a reason. God is the reason!

CHAPTER

Chapter Three

DEFILING THE TEMPLE

The temples of old became defiled when the dedicated purpose of the temple was changed and tampered with by unholy hands. The sanctuaries were dedicated unto God as His dwelling place and as houses of worship and sacrifice. It was within the courtyards of the tabernacles and the temples that daily offerings were made unto God. When the purpose of the house was breached, the temple became profaned and was declared by God as defiled. Profaned means to be polluted, stained, defiled, prostituted, and to break one's word. The profaning of the temple happened, for example, when idols were introduced into the courts and within the holy sanctuary.

That they have committed adultery, and blood is in their hands, and with their idols have they committed adultery, and have also caused their sons, whom they bare unto me, to pass for them through the fire, to devour them. Moreover this they have done unto me: they have defiled my sanctuary in the same day, and have profaned my sabbaths. (Ezekiel 23:37-38).

Idolatry is spiritual adultery. Adultery is committed by breaking the marriage covenant. Adultery is the sexual joining of two people where at least one of the parties is dedicated and committed to another. Adultery defiles and profanes the marriage covenant. God told His people that they had committed adultery by setting up idols in the temple. The covenant with God was broken. The dedicated purpose of the temple was therefore altered.

Defilement of the temple also took place when the holy dedicated places became a mixture of that which God required and that which man desired.

Her priests have violated my law, and have profaned mine holy things: they have put no difference between the holy and profane, neither have they shewed difference between the unclean and the clean, and have hid their eyes from my sabbaths, and I am profaned among them. (Ezekiel 22:26)

What happened in the days of Ezekiel is still happening today. Priests of God, the spiritual leaders of our day, have failed to put a difference between that which is clean and acceptable unto God and that which is defiled, unclean, unholy and unacceptable to God. The modern church is full of the violation of God's instructions concerning holiness.

The world has crept into the church culture. Godliness is no longer the norm or the accepted measuring rod by which a Christian's actions and life are measured. Rather, the culture of the world now dominates the Church. No distinguishable difference is made between the life of a Christian and the life of a heathen. No difference is made between that which is and that which is not acceptable to God. That which is clean and that which is unclean is accepted as the same. Holiness and unholiness are mixed together in the same pot. That which is evil is called good, and that which is good is called evil.

Woe unto them that call evil good, and good evil; that put darkness for light, and light for darkness; that put bitter for sweet, and sweet for bitter! (Isaiah 5:20)

In this generation, people are encouraged to live as they wish. Serving one's own appetites is not only encouraged, but also endorsed. Instead of God's Word being the lamp of guidance, people's own preferences and desires have become their guide. Fences of restraint have been removed. If anyone should be so bold as to raise questions concerning morality, holiness and purity, they are considered politically incorrect. Some even go so far as to accuse the speakers of truth as being those who are the spreaders of hate speech. This trend within the Church is a part of the prophetic promise and a sign of the end-times.

This know also, that in the last days perilous times shall come. For men shall be lovers of their own selves, covetous, boasters, proud, blasphemers, disobedient to parents, unthankful, unholy, Without natural affection, trucebreakers, false accusers, incontinent, fierce, despisers of those that are good, Traitors, heady, highminded, lovers of pleasures more than lovers of God; Having a form of godliness, but denying the power thereof: from such turn away. (2 Timothy 3:1-5)

These words, written two thousand years ago by the Apostle Paul to his son in the Faith, Timothy, are a living reality in the world today. Currently, we see a form of godliness that is actually anti-god and self-serving. There is no difference between purity and impurity, good and evil, and light and darkness. In general, the church world has become a mixture of Christian persuasion and Paganism. Both eastern religions and the customs of the world have been integrated into worship unto God. We are witnessing the same thing today that took place in the days of Ezekiel.

And he brought me into the inner court of the LORD's house, and, behold, at the door of the temple of the LORD, between the porch and the altar, were about five and twenty men, with their backs toward the temple of the LORD, and their faces toward the east; and they worshipped the sun toward the east. (Ezekiel 8:16)

In Ezekiel's vision, he saw the leadership, the priesthood, standing within the inner court of God's holy temple worshipping the sun. Their backs were turned towards the holy sanctuary as they faced the East. The practices of the priesthood were a mixture of God's Law and Paganism. The temple was profaned and defiled due to their twisted form of worship. As those who were called unto the service of the priesthood stood within the inner court of God's holy temple, with their backs turned towards the temple, they simultaneously turned their faces towards the East in worship of the traditions of the heathen. What a mixture! It was not long after this that God's glory and His residing presence departed from the temple (Ezekiel 10).

History is repeating itself. Churches are more like night clubs today than holy dedicated places of worship. The worship service is no longer about man serving God. Rather, it is about man serving himself. The mode of the day is to create an environment where everyone can feel comfortable and without conviction. Worship now revolves around creating an atmosphere. Entertainment has become the new form of worship. Sermons have turned into motivational speeches with the goal of causing the audience to feel good about themselves. The appetites of man dictate what should be served in the Church.

(For many walk, of whom I have told you often, and now tell you even weeping, that they are the enemies of the cross of Christ: Whose end is destruction, whose God is their belly, and whose glory is in their shame, who mind earthly things.) (Philippians 3:18-19).

When the belly, which is man's self-serving appetite, becomes the god that is served, then the dedicated purpose of the vessel is broken; the temple becomes profaned; and the commitment to purpose is damaged. This is idolatry and spiritual adultery.

What? know ye not that he which is joined to an

harlot is one body? for two, saith he, shall be one flesh. But he that is joined unto the Lord is one spirit. Flee fornication. Every sin that a man doeth is without the body; but he that committeth fornication sinneth against his own body. What? know ye not that your body is the temple of the Holy Ghost which is in you, which ye have of God, and ye are not your own? For ye are bought with a price: therefore glorify God in your body, and in your spirit, which are God's (1 Corinthians 6:16-20).

These are powerful and strong words written by the Apostle Paul to the church in Corinth. The central focus of these words is the fact that our bodies are the temple of the Holy Ghost. Joining the temple to that which is unclean and using the body in immoral ways and practices are in reality defiling the temple of God. We are not called unto such *doing.* This is not who we are called and chosen to *be.*

Paul cautioned the Corinthian church to flee fornication. Fornication means to be highly fed, wanton (sexually immodest, lacking discipline), adultery, idolatry, and to play the harlot.

Let's take a look at verse eighteen again from the HCSB translation:

Run from sexual immorality! "Every sin a person can commit is outside the body." On the contrary, the person who is sexually immoral sins against his own body. (1 Corinthians 6:18) HCSB

Fornication reaches far beyond the physical acts of sex. Just look around you. Almost everything in the secular world is connected in some way to sex. Paul is speaking about sexual immodesty, *highly feeding* sexual appetites, and a lack of discipline in one's moral conduct.

All "committed" sins, or sins of deeds and actions as referred to in the verse above, are committed externally or *by* the body. However, sexual misconduct is a sin *against* the body, or against the temple of God. What we do with our bodies, the manner in which we present our bodies, and the way in which we use our bodies, is of utmost importance to God. Our bodies are His sanctuary. Whatever the sanctuary is joined to becomes a part of *'the sanctuary'*. This is why God is so particular as to what we do with our bodies. Paul, therefore ends I Corinthians chapter six by saying that we are to glorify God with our bodies and with our spirits, as they are God's.

It is God's will that His people uphold moral purity both *within,* and *without.* True holiness is in maintaining a vessel, a sanctuary, a temple, and a house that is dedicated and set apart unto God. This simply means that the house is kept for its dedicated and specific purpose and calling. We are not to join the temple to that which is defiled and unclean.

And what agreement hath the temple of God with idols? for ye are the temple of the living God; as God hath said, I will dwell in them, and walk in them; and I will be their God, and they shall be my people. Wherefore come out from among them, and be ye separate, saith the Lord, and touch not the unclean thing; and I will receive you (2 Corinthians 6:16-17).

The temple of God has always been called a *holy place*. God requires for His dwelling to be free from filth and grime. He demands that His house be a dedicated sanctuary in which His glory and presence can reside. The same God that dwelt among men in buildings of stone under the Old Covenant now dwells within the hearts of men under the New Covenant. His desire to dwell in a dedicated place has not changed because He has not changed.

The following scriptures make reference to God's temple being holy: Psalm 5:7, 11:4, 65:4, 79:1,

138:2 / Jonah 2:4,7 / Micah 1:2 / Habakkuk 2:20 / Ephesians 2:21.

It was forbidden for the temple of God to enter into any form of league, confederacy, covenant or agreement with idolaters or idols. Naturally, when we think of idols, we imagine a little Buddha propped up in the corner of the room or possibly some other form of graven imagery. However, close examination of our own personal temples will reveal a shocking reality. Within us, within the human heart, within the place where God desires to dwell, and within the sanctuary where God demands dedication unto Himself, we find all manner of immoral images and idols that we bow to on a perpetual basis.

If anyone is halfway sincere and halfway honest with themselves, they will acknowledge that bowing to all manner of mental images is a continuous practice of the human heart. Whether we are conscious of it or not, humans dedicate their lives and existence to idols, images and ideas that have been formed within the mind and heart. Hence, our daily lives widely revolve around serving these images and bowing to their cause. This is idolatry – and yes, our temple, our hearts, and our minds are filled with it! True holiness is maintaining a temple void of idols.

For they themselves shew of us what manner of entering in we had unto you, and how ye turned to God from idols to serve the living and true God; And to wait for his Son from heaven, whom he raised from the dead, even Jesus, which delivered us from the wrath to come (1 Thessalonians 1:9-10).

We can never fulfill the ultimate purpose for which Jesus died until we turn from idols. Our lives can never *be holiness unto the LORD*, until we turn from idols. God's residing presence will not fill our hearts until we divorce ourselves from idol images. As a matter of fact, destruction awaits the temple that is occupied by idols.

If any man defile the temple of God, him shall God destroy; for the temple of God is holy, which temple ye are. (1 Corinthians 3:17)

These are harsh words given by the Apostle Paul. Many would argue that such language does not belong in the New Testament era of Grace. It is not politically correct to talk about the destruction of the temple, when the temple being referred to is, 'us'. Yet, in this scripture, we see a message that is given in the New Testament dispensation to a New Testament Church announcing destruction on the temple that is defiled by idolatry. What are we to make of this? In the context of this verse, the meaning of the word, "destroy", is not implying eternal damnation. Rather, the destruction means to pine or to waste away, to shrivel or to wither, to be spoiled and ruined (especially by moral influences), and to be corrupted and defiled.

The vessel that is called to be set apart for the presence of God, can never reach its calling or potential, whilst breaking away from God's purpose due to serving idols.

In my forty years of ministry, I have been privileged to minister to countless people all over the world. The sad reality, however, is that everywhere I have been, I have seen souls who are wasting away, spoiled, ruined and withered in their spiritual lives. One of the main reasons for this is that they do not choose to clean up their temple. Instead, they chose the defilement of idols over God's dwelling presence. Hence, they discover that both their natural and spiritual lives are surrounded with destruction. What a waste!

When I was a young minister, I had the privilege of pastoring a young man named Joe (I have used an alias name). Joe had an incredible call of God upon his life, and he was gifted on many levels. God had blessed him with an amazing talent to play music on a number of instruments. He also had a tremendous capacity for the Word of God. Joe carried a God given anointing that few have. He was mightily anointed to minister in spiritual gifts, and had a powerful personal calling upon his life. But, Joe would not stop messing around with the world. Joe reminded me of Samson of old.

Joe was warned, over and over again, by the Spirit and the Word of God to clean up His life. God drew him, called him, blessed him, and continuously convicted him of the wrongs that he had invited into his world. In spite, he refused to deal with and divorce himself of the idols that he had bowed to continuously. Joe gave his temple to sex, drugs, and alcohol. He committed all of this in secret. Few, if anyone, knew of his behavior. As his pastor, I knew. I warned him, pleaded with him, and prayed with him. Instead, Joe chose to serve his own appetites rather than to be a temple that was dedicated unto God.

One day, when Joe was traveling he pulled over to the side of the road to check on a rattling sound that he heard coming from the rear of his car. As he opened his car door and stepped out, a huge truck came speeding by. The driver of the truck had not seen Joe open his car door. He plowed right into him. Joe was thrown high into the air and upon landing he was instantly decapitated.

Upon investigation, the police discovered hard drugs and alcohol in Joe's car. This, dear reader, is a tragic story of a wasted life. This brings tears to my eyes as I relive this traumatic experience and share this tragedy. Ruin and destruction followed Joe. He was mightily called to be a living temple of God, filled to overflowing with God's residing glory and presence as manifested through the gifts and the anointing upon his life. Serving the idols of his own appetites became his downfall and ruin. This is only one story of a multitude that I could share of temples that have been wasted.

Don't play with God! Do not play with His mercy and grace. Do not play with the house that He calls His temple. God is not mocked. As a man sows, so shall he reap (Galatians 6:7).

*And we know that the Son of God is come, and hath given us an understanding, that we may know him that is true, and we are in him that is true, even in his Son Jesus Christ. This is the true God, and eternal life. Little children, **keep yourselves from idols**. Amen (1 John 5:20-21). (Highlight added by the author)*

CHAPTER

Chapter Four

A HOLY NATION

Holiness is a fundamental truth that is to be practiced by all believers who desire to walk with God and who long to pursue a dedicated life unto Him. Living a life of holiness and dedication is not only reserved for an elite group, or for those who are called to a particular service or ministry. Holiness is not ordained for the ordained. Holiness is not prescribed for those who occupy a particular role or status within the church. Holiness is a requirement for all of God's people, whether great or small, young or old, whether serving in the ministry or not.

Since all believers are called and purposed by God as living temples in which the Spirit and presence of God reside, all believers are therefore called unto holiness. God has ordained His people as a royal priesthood and a *holy nation*. Holiness does not pertain to a few within the nation. It pertains to all of the nation!

But ye are a chosen generation, a royal priesthood, an holy nation, a peculiar people; that ye should shew forth the praises of him who hath called you out of darkness into his marvellous light: Which in time past were not a people, but are now the people of God: which had not obtained mercy, but now have obtained mercy (1 Peter 2:9-10).

Man, in his attempt to be holy, has devised all manner of religious rituals, laws and guidelines. These religious formats have been established in an effort to create a boundary. By living within these boundaries man attempts to make himself acceptable unto God. Yet, all of mankind's attempts to perform religious rites are futile if his heart is not set apart and dedicated unto God. A dedicated life has little, if anything, to do with observing a ritualistic lifestyle. Performing a multitude of ceremonious deeds without a heart that is dedicated to God simply produces a Pharisaical and hypocritical spirit.

Woe unto you, scribes and Pharisees, hypocrites! for ye make clean the outside of the cup and of the platter, but within they are full of extortion and excess. Thou blind Pharisee, cleanse first that which is within the cup and platter, that the outside of them may be clean also. Woe unto you, scribes and Pharisees, hypocrites! for ye are like unto whited sepulchres, which indeed appear beautiful outward, but are within full of dead men's bones, and of all uncleanness. Even so ye also outwardly appear righteous unto men, but within ye are full of hypocrisy and iniquity (Matthew 23:25-28)

Spoken by Jesus to the religious people of His day, these words are severe and jarring to the senses. However, what the Master spoke two thousand years ago still rings true to this generation. The question is not, *'How do I appear?'* or *'How do I look?'* The question should rather be, *'Am I dedicated?* Is my life truly set apart unto God from within?'

Dedication and set apartness unto God, precedes all moral behavior.

The fruit of a dedicated life will be moral purity within and without. A life that is not dedicated unto God may externally appear right, and even behave correctly, and yet, that life will not *be* right before God.

Holiness could not be better summed up than in the words that were written by the Apostle Paul to the Hebrews:

For this is the covenant that I will make with the house of Israel after those days, saith the Lord; I will put my laws into their mind, and write them in their hearts: and I will be to them a God, and they shall be to me a people (Hebrews 8:10).

This verse describes a dedicated and a set apart life. It describes people who have God's living Law within their minds and hearts. Christ, the living Word of God, is God's living Law. The people of God are those who honor the Almighty as their God in all that they are. They are His people, set apart from all others and all else, dedicated unto Him. This is holiness!

God said that His covenant would be made with the whole House of Israel, and not just with a few tribes. The covenant was to be with the whole nation. God has called all of His people unto holiness. No matter your calling and no matter the ministry in which you serve, you are called unto holiness.

A number of large religious movements call themselves *holiness movements.* Some organizations tack the word *holiness* onto the name of their church so as to identify themselves as a *holiness movement*. In many of these cases, we see whited sepulchers, rather than dedication unto God.

Many believers have been taught to look a certain way, dress in a certain way, behave in a certain manner, and present themselves according to a particular dress code, format or *religious fashion*. I am not inferring that God does not require our appearance to reflect holiness. He most certainly does.* However, we can do all of the outward works and perform all of the religious rituals, and still remain as filthy as the drunk in the gutter. Why? Because the inside is dirty. What we do must correspond to who we are. Outward attempts towards holiness are futile, meaningless, and powerless if the heart is not involved. This is what the Apostle Paul referred to as a form of godliness that possessed no power.

Having a form of godliness, but denying the power thereof: from such turn away. (2 Timothy 3:5)

The word dedicated in the Webster's Dictionary means: (of a person) devoted to a task or purpose, having single-minded loyalty or integrity: (of a thing) exclusively allocated to or intended for a particular service or purpose.

*(Dressing To Please The Lord – by Paul M Hanssen – available on amazon.com in Kindle and paperback).

If we, as believers, dedicate, consecrate, and set ourselves apart unto God, then *our lives will **be** holiness unto the LORD*. Passive holiness will lead us to active holiness. Being dedicated within our hearts will lead us to doing deeds of holy active living. The manner in which we live our lives and conduct ourselves will reveal our dedication unto God. In contrast, without such dedication, our lives will reflect the lack thereof through our deeds. No matter how much you may attempt to present yourself as holy, ultimately the facade will fade and the mask will fall off. True holiness cannot be maintained without devotion!

Go and cry in the ears of Jerusalem, saying, Thus saith the LORD; I remember thee, the kindness of thy youth, the love of thine espousals, when thou wentest after me in the wilderness, in a land that was not sown. Israel was holiness unto the LORD, and the firstfruits of his increase: all that devour him shall offend; evil shall come upon them, saith the LORD (Jeremiah 2:2-3).

At the command of God, Jeremiah spoke these words over Jerusalem. God was reminding His people of the early days of their freedom from slavery, when they were dedicated to follow Him. At that time and season, the nation walked after God, they desired Him even in a wilderness that was undesirable. God said, in so many words, ***at that time you were holiness unto the LORD***. In that season of their journey, the nation was dedicated and set apart unto the LORD. God continues to desire such devotion from His people.

The reason that the Church lacks moral character, purity and cleanliness is because the Church, in general, is no longer dedicated, hallowed and set apart unto God. The effect of this is a lack of holiness and hence, a lack of moral standards. God desires to dwell in and among a dedicated, hallowed people. He longs to reside in a temple that is set apart unto Him.

The following diagram illustrates the dedication unto purpose, and the fulfilling of the purpose in being dedicated.

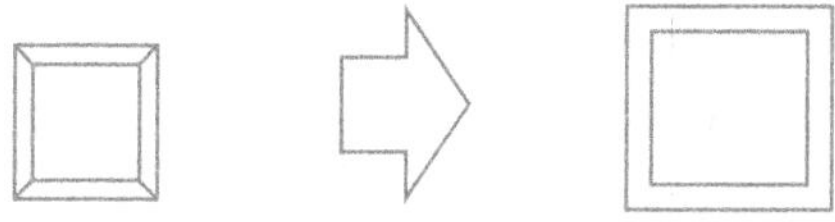

OBJECT / DEDICATED UNTO / PURPOSE

Try to picture yourself as the *object*. Then, picture God as the *purpose*. Lastly, picture *holiness* as the *dedication unto* the purpose. If the object should change its form and depart from its intended purpose, then it could no longer be dedicated unto its purpose. The object would no longer fit into that for which it was designed.

For example, a hammer is created to build and to construct. A hammer is made with the specific purpose of being a constructive tool. However, a hammer can also be used to murder a victim. Therefore, if a hammer is used to kill, instead of to build, its purpose becomes defiled and contaminated. The hammer is no longer a tool, but instead becomes a weapon. The object no longer fits into its intended purpose.

This same principle applies to holiness. Holiness is dedication unto God. True dedication and holiness are the bridge that joins man to his intended purpose. Without maintaining inner dedication unto God, mankind is not able to fulfill the purpose for which he was created. The reason for our existence is God! Never forget, God is the purpose! He is the reason for all existence!

Behold, I build an house to the name of the LORD my God, to dedicate it to him, and to burn before him sweet incense, and for the continual shewbread, and for the burnt offerings morning and evening, on the sabbaths, and on the new moons, and on the solemn feasts of the LORD our God. This is an ordinance for ever to Israel. And the house which I build is great: for great is our God above all gods (2 Chronicles 2:4-5).

As already mentioned, the Hebrew word for *dedicate* is *kaw-doshe / kaw-dash* which means holy, hallowed and set apart. I cannot emphasize enough that this is the type of house in which God desires to dwell. This is the type of vessel that God desires to use. Many people in this generation want to be used by God, but they do not want to be dedicated.

The temple that Solomon constructed was built with a purpose in mind. God was the purpose. The temple was erected to house God's presence and glory. All of the daily activities within the outer court, the inner court, and within the sanctuary proper, took place because of the temple's dedicated purpose. When the temple was defiled and lost its dedication, God left the house. The temple no longer fulfilled its purpose.

Read the following scriptures in your Bible to discover the succession of God's glory presence as it departed from His temple house.

- *Ezekiel 9:3* - God's Glory lifted from off of the Ark between the Cherubim.
- *Ezekiel 10:4* - God's Glory went and stood over the

threshold of the temple house.

- *Ezekiel 10:18-19* - God's Glory then lifted off of the threshold and proceeded to the door of the east gate.
- *Ezekiel 11:23* - God's glory then moved to the mountain on the east side of the city before taking flight and departing Jerusalem.

Take note as to how slowly and reluctantly the glory presence of the LORD departed from His own temple house. His departure was neither sudden nor abrupt. He only departed after giving multiple warnings. This reminds me of Samson. (Judges chapters 13-16). God's presence and power dwelt upon him, but Samson began to allow his appetites to lead him astray. In spite, God remained with him. Samson may have felt that since the presence of God was still with him, he remained in God's favor. This was not the case, however. Even though he was warned over and over again, he failed to take heed and turn from his sinful ways. However, his reluctance to heed God's warnings eventually caught up with him. Unbeknown to him, God's presence departed. Samson was left without the power or strength to fight against the enemies that continuously sought to destroy him. Believe me when I say, God will leave His house, but not without warning.

God's purpose has always been to dwell among His people. He was, therefore, in no hurry to leave. God's glory hesitated in hopes that the people would repent and once again dedicate the house, and themselves unto Him. But God's glory eventually departed because His house had lost the dedication unto Him. It had lost holiness. The temple that was once dedicated unto God became a place that was now dedicated unto idols.

Know ye not that ye are the temple of God, and that the Spirit of God dwelleth in you? If any man defile the temple of God, him shall God destroy; for the temple of God is holy, which temple ye are. (1 Corinthians 3:16-17)

In whom all the building fitly framed together groweth unto an holy temple in the Lord: In whom ye also are builded together for an habitation of God through the Spirit. (Ephesians 2:21-22 / see Romans 6:22)

For God hath not called us unto uncleanness, but unto holiness. (1 Thessalonians 4:7).

As a people who are redeemed and purchased by the blood of Jesus, we are called to live holy lives that are set apart and dedicated unto God. God's people are not called to live unto themselves. They are not called to live their lives dedicated unto the lusts of their flesh. They are not called to live to the world. They are not called to impurity and immorality. They are not called to walk as the heathen do. They are not called to be governed by their appetites and cravings for self-satisfaction. God's people are called unto holiness!

God is dedicated and hallowed unto His purpose, unto His will and unto His holy Name. He desires to dwell among and within a people who are dedicated and hallowed unto Him. Such dedication creates within the lives of His people moral purity and cleanliness of body, soul and spirit.

My question to the Church today is not, "Are you holy?" My question is rather, "Unto what and unto whom are you dedicated?"

CHAPTER FIVE

Chapter Five

HOLINESS OR SELF-RIGHTEOUSNESS

Self-righteousness is a stench in the nostrils of God. Self-righteousness is the result of people doing holiness without being holy. Such behavior in the life of a believer has the potential to create a *holier than thou attitude.*

Which say, Stand by thyself, come not near to me; for I am holier than thou. These are a smoke in my nose, a fire that burneth all the day (Isaiah 65:5).

The 'holier than thou' attitude is like a continuous smoke rising in the nostrils of God. Self-righteousness is condemned throughout God's Word. God hates self-righteousness!

One day, Jesus was speaking to a group of people who considered themselves to be righteous. He told the parable of two men who went to the temple to pray. One man was a publican, the other was a Pharisee. The Pharisee prayed great and grandiose words proclaiming himself to be better than others. Pharisees always adorned themselves in religious attire according to their rituals and laws. Here, the Pharisee stood at the temple adorned in all of his honor and with a bold, loud voice announced his righteousness for all to see and hear.

On the other hand, Jesus spoke of the publican. Publicans were tax collectors and known thieves. They were considered unjust, unfair, and certainly unholy, and yet it was the publican who came before the temple of God with contrition, brokenness and repentance. He beat his chest and would not so much as lift up his eyes to behold the holy temple. He confessed that he was a sinner, unclean, and impure.

Jesus informed the self-righteous listeners to whom He spoke that it was indeed the publican that went home justified, not the Pharisee. Looking right, sounding right, and performing the religious rituals did nothing for the Pharisee but to cause God to turn His face away. But brokenness of the spirit and repentance of the heart brought true righteousness into the life of the publican. (Matthew 18:10-14).

Deeds or acts of outward holiness, modesty, and separation are well pleasing to the Lord. God desires of His people to present themselves in a modest, non-sensuous, and unprovocative manner. Those professing Godliness should be mindful of the way that their bodies are presented.

 In like manner also, that women adorn themselves in modest apparel, with shamefacedness and sobriety; not with broided hair, or gold, or pearls, or costly array; But (which becometh women professing godliness) with good works (1 Thessalonians 2:9-10).

These commands, of course, do not only apply to woman, but also to men. We are all called to consider the manner in which we present ourselves as vessels of God's glory and as temples that house His presence.

However, among some believers there is nothing as twisted and as misused as the practice of outward standards. In many religious affiliations, dress codes are used to measure a member's maturity or spiritual stature. Outward standards have also become a religious fashion. Looking a certain way is used as a tool of identification. In other words, if you don't look right, then you don't belong with us. This type of outward holiness breeds spiritual pride and causes 'the saints' to lift their hearts in arrogance against others who do not live up to the status quo. This, however, is not true holiness! This type of *holier than thou* attitude is disgusting and repugnant to God. This is the true definition of a Pharisee.

When Jesus walked among men, He ministered with such passion, compassion, forgiveness and grace. He healed the sick, raised the dead, cleansed the lepers, forgave the sinners, cast out devils and fed the multitudes. However, His ministry had another side to it. The other side of His ministry was fierce and often administered with holy anger and harsh language. If Jesus preached some of His sermons among us today, it would be considered by many as hate speech. This harsh tone was observed when He spoke to the religious people of His day, namely the Pharisees.

The name, Pharisee, actually means to be separated. The Pharisees were separatists. They were secluded from all others who did not see as they saw, believe as they believed, or who did not observe the law as they did. Their separation was not unto God, however. They were separated unto their religious beliefs and unto a religious system.

The Pharisees maintained strict beliefs in the Torah, the Law of God that was given to Moses. But, the Pharisees also believed in the Oral Law.

The Oral Law was a compilation of traditions that were passed down from generation to generation. These traditions had no basis in God's written Law. They were, in fact, man made and man enforced. The Pharisees maintained a long list of 613 laws. Anyone who did not believe in the 613 laws and who lived differently than what the laws demanded, were dogs and sinners in their eyes.

It is this separatist spirit that Jesus fought so vehemently against. Throughout His three-and-a-half-year ministry, Jesus was continuously at odds with the Pharisees.

Then came to Jesus scribes and Pharisees, which were of Jerusalem, saying, Why do thy disciples transgress the tradition of the elders? For they wash not their hands when they eat bread. But he answered and said unto them, Why do ye also transgress the commandment of God by your tradition? (Matthew 15:1-3).

The Scribes and the Pharisees held their traditions in higher esteem than the Word of God itself. They lived their lives according to their traditions. Yet, they were actually transgressing the Word of God with their traditions. It is important for us to take note of this.

We should all ask ourselves this question, "Are our beliefs founded upon the solid Word of God, or is our worship, behavior, lifestyle, and service based on the traditions that have been passed down from generation to generation within our church?"

Over the years, I have confronted many pastors concerning certain practices performed in their churches. Many of these practices had no scriptural basis. The response that I have received all too often has been, "We have always done it this way." In other words, the traditions of the church that had been passed down from generation to generation had become more important than the Word of God itself.

Religious traditions have a way of producing self-righteousness when they are not grounded in the Word of Truth! Holiness, when based on tradition only, will produce self-righteousness. Self-righteousness, in turn, will ultimately lead to spiritual death. A tradition is something that has been performed for so long that it carries the weight of the Law.

Saying, The scribes and the Pharisees sit in Moses' seat: All therefore whatsoever they bid you observe, that observe and do; but do not ye after their works: for they say, and do not. For they bind heavy burdens and grievous to be borne, and lay them on men's shoulders; but they themselves will not move them with one of their fingers. But all their works they do for to be seen of men: they make broad their phylacteries, and enlarge the borders of their garments (Matthew 23:2-5).

The religious rituals that were placed upon the people by the Pharisees and Scribes were too heavy for the people to bear. These rules produced spiritual death, fruitlessness, and spiritual barrenness.

We must be cautious in our attempts to live our lives as being separated unto God. We must do so as unto Him, and not as unto a religion or a religious practice. We are called to be separated. But, our separation must be our dedication unto God, and not a dedication to a church, or to a doctrine, or to a particular format, or to a church fashion. Such dedication is nothing but dead religious practice; all of which produce the spirit of self-righteousness and spiritual death.

CHAPTER SIX

Chapter Six

THE HOLINESS OF GOD

When we consider how much of the person, character, nature and presence of God are wrapped in holiness, then it behooves us to consider how we too should aspire to be as He is.

- God is glorious in holiness
  Exodus 15:11
- God is to be worshipped in the beauty of holiness.
  1 Chronicles 16:29 / Psalm 29:2
- Thank God at the remembrance of His holiness.
  Psalm 30:4
- God's throne is holiness
  Psalm 47:8
- The mountain of God is holiness
  Psalm 48:1 /Jeremiah 31:23/
- God speaks in holiness
  Psalm 60:6 / Psalm 108:7
- God swears by His own holiness
  Psalm 89:35 / Amos 4:2
- God's name is Holy
  Psalm 111:9 / Luke 1:49
- The way of God is a highway of holiness

Isaiah 35:8
- The courts of the LORD are holiness
  Isaiah 62:9
- The habitation of God is holiness
  Isaiah 63:15
- God's words are words of holiness
  Jeremiah 23:9
- The Spirit of God is holy
  Ephesians 4:30

Every aspect of God is holy, dedicated, appointed, set apart, and consecrated unto His holy will and purpose. There is nothing about God that is not holy. He is holiness through and through. This is what God desires of His people. He also wants us to be holy as He is holy!

R.C. Sproul writes this about the holiness of God:
"The Bible says that God is holy, holy, holy. Not that He is merely holy, or even holy, holy. He is holy, holy, holy. The Bible never says that God is love, love, love, or mercy, mercy, mercy, or wrath, wrath, wrath, or justice, justice, justice. It does say that He is holy, holy, holy, the whole earth is full of His glory."

"When the Bible calls God holy it means primarily that God is transcendentally separate. He is so far above and beyond us that He seems almost totally foreign to us. To be holy is to be 'other,' to be

different in a special way. The same basic meaning is used when the word holy is applied to earthly things."

God is totally separated and set-a-part from all others. He is absolutely dedicated and hallowed unto His own purpose. Nothing can change who He is. He is, therefore, holy!

There is much more to be said about the holiness of God and God's desire for His people to be holy as He is holy. However, the fundamental truth concerning holiness is that we aspire, desire and aim to live our lives dedicated, consecrated, hallowed, and separated unto God. The pursuit of His likeness should be our highest and ultimate goal. This produces holiness. A life dedicated unto God is a life that is set apart unto Him.

R.C Sproul's dissertation concerning God's holiness mentions love, mercy, wrath, and justice. These are all attributes of God. God is love, just like God is holy. However, what sets God's love apart from all other expressions of love is the fact that the love of God is holy love. There is no love like His love. His love is pure and dedicated unto His purpose, undefiled and unwavering. His love is holy!

Mankind classifies many of his actions as deeds of

love. Many churches and Christians profess to have the love of God working in their midst. However, should someone contradict them or shun their beliefs, these same professors of 'love' are quick to retrieve their deeds and expressions of love. This said 'love' quickly turns to resistance, and in some instances even to hatred.

Man's love is biased, tainted, prejudiced, and self-serving. God's love is holy because His love is dedicated unto His purpose, and hence it is unchanging. If the love that we express to others is not birthed from true dedication unto God, then it is merely a display of human affection, not to be confused with the love of God. Human affection does not stand the test of rejection. Human affection wavers when it is not responded to in a manner that one feels deserving of. Human affection will pick and choose unto whom it will display its fervor.

The love of God does not act in this manner. God's love is holy. It is unshakable because it is dedicated unto truth and purpose. Do you see the difference?

Every attribute of the nature and character of God is birthed from His holiness. His mercy is holy. His justice and judgements are holy. His wrath is holy. There is nothing about God that is not holy.

Holiness is the very center and core essence of God's nature. God is holy!

CHAPTER

Chapter Seven

PASSIVE HOLINESS

True Biblical holiness is first and foremost passive, not active. In the previous chapters, we have discussed what it means to *be* holy. The *'being'* aspect of holiness is passive holiness. Passive holiness is not based upon what a person does. Instead, it is based on what or who a person *is*. Nobody can be actively holy without passive holiness.

In Martin Luther's commentary on Galatians written in 1535, he writes:

Christian holiness is not active but passive. Therefore let no one call himself holy on the basis of his way of life or his works... Such works, of course, are holy, and God strictly demands them of us; but they do not make us holy. You and I are holy; the church, the city, and the people are holy - not on the basis of their own holiness, but on the basis of a holiness not their own, not by an active holiness, but by a passive holiness.

Even though Luther had a different idea as to what passive holiness was, his words, nonetheless, scream a huge amen in my soul.

God, Himself, is not holy on the basis of what He does. He is holy on the basis of who He is. He *is* dedicated, hallowed, and consecrated to His own will, purpose and great Name. God is God, and God is holy because He *'is'* God. Also, God is love because love is the essence of who He is. God is not love because of what He does. He does not do acts of love in order to be a God of love. God does not have to perform any act to make Himself the God of love. God *is* love because of who He *is*. As a result, what He is produces what He does. The fact that He is love causes Him to do works of love. In like manner, God is holy because that is who and what He is.

It is unto this kind of holiness that God has called His people! He has called us to be holy as He is holy. This means being dedicated and consecrated unto His will, purpose and name, just as He is. I may come across as being repetitive and redundant, however I am endeavoring to drive home a principle in hopes that the reader will never forget.

Passive holiness is received and gained only

through Jesus Christ, by faith. He is the only source of true holiness. Passive holiness is obtained by faith in that which Jesus has already accomplished. Without faith no man can please God. No matter how hard you attempt to be holy; no matter how many works you try to do, you cannot be holy without faith. Dedication and consecration unto Him are only accomplished by faith. Believing in the Holy One makes us holy. This is passive holiness.

This same principle and operation of truth is experienced in salvation. Outward works cannot save anybody. The sinner is not saved by attempting to be a good person. No amount of good deeds or visible works can redeem. Only by faith can a sinner be saved.

For by grace are ye saved through faith; and that not of yourselves: it is the gift of God: Not of works, lest any man should boast. (Ephesians 2:8-9)

If salvation were accomplished by man's deeds, he would be able to boast in his own works and means by which he was saved. Salvation begins in the heart as passive faith. Passive faith believes in what Jesus accomplished on the cross of Calvary. However, the faith in Jesus' work of redemption becomes a visible display of a changed life. The passive faith within is outwardly seen by deeds of active faith. After all, faith without works is dead.

(James 2:17,20).

In like manner, this is also how holiness works. Active holiness is an outward manifestation of a heart that is full of faith in the Holy One. Faith means persuasion. To be persuaded is to be convinced about something without wavering. Persuasion does not falter. Dedication is realized when unwavering persuasion grabs the heart. This kind of faith in God leads the believer to active holiness. Unfortunately, the Church today is full of people who are not persuaded. Their faith in God is shallow, and as a result the display of holiness in their lives is also shallow or non-existent.

The temple was hallowed and made holy by dedication. It was not the works that were done in the temple that made it a holy place. It was what the temple was dedicated unto that made it holy. The daily sacrifices and ordinances that were carried out in the tabernacle and temple did not *make* the house holy. Rather, they were performed *because* the house *was* holy.

Woe unto you, ye blind guides, which say, Whosoever shall swear by the temple, it is nothing; but whosoever shall swear by the gold of the temple, he is a debtor! Ye fools and blind: for whether is greater, the gold, or the temple that sanctifieth the gold? And, Whosoever shall swear by the altar, it is nothing; but whosoever sweareth by the gift that is upon it, he is guilty. Ye fools and blind: for whether is greater, the gift, or the altar that sanctifieth the gift? (Matthew 23:16-19)

When rebuking the Scribes and the Pharisees, Jesus made His point very clear concerning their twisted view on what they considered relevant, important, and holy. The Scribes and Pharisees believed that the golden vessels used in their sacrificial ordinances, along with the sacrifices that were made upon the altar in the temple, were more holy than the temple itself. Jesus called them blind. They could not see that it was not the fulfilling of the ordinances nor the sacrifices that were made on the altar that caused the temple to be holy. Instead, it was the temple that made the gold holy, and it was the altar that sanctified and made the sacrifice holy.

Unfortunately, many Christians live their lives believing in the same manner of twisted theology as did the Scribes and Pharisees. Many believe that they are able to make themselves holy by offering sacrifices and performing the correct daily religious rituals. No, dear saint of God, the opposite is the truth. It is by the temple *being* holy and dedicated unto its purpose, that the works, sacrifices, and acts of obedience performed therein are sanctified and made holy. When your vessel is dedicated unto God from within, then the One whom you are dedicated unto by persuasion, sanctifies your works and sacrifices, and not vice versa.

The altar sanctified and hallowed the sacrifice; it was not the sacrifice that hallowed the altar. The altar was initially dedicated and set apart unto sacrifice. Therefore, everything that touched the altar was hallowed. When our lives are dedicated and set apart unto God from within, from the heart, by our faith and persuasion, then our works and sacrifices are holy. Yet, we live years of our lives performing outward deeds and sacrifices in an effort to gain the reality of holiness. We need a transforming of our minds to take place, so that we may truly live a life of dedicated holiness.

Passive holiness is holiness that we do not produce by ourselves. Works and sacrifices cannot produce passive holiness. It is a faith matter; a matter of persuasion; a heart commitment; an internal affair, and a solid unwavering stand that is made.

To the end he may stablish your hearts unblameable in holiness before God, even our Father, at the coming of our Lord Jesus Christ with all his saints (1 Thessalonians 3:13).

I would like to end this chapter with words written by J.C. Ryle:

"Holiness is the habit of being of one mind with God, according as we find His mind described in Scripture. It is the habit of agreeing in God's judgment, hating what He hates, loving what He loves, and measuring everything in this world by the standard of His Word".

My soul says, 'Yes' to these powerful words. Holiness is the habit of being of one mind with God. This, in my opinion, describes passive holiness. Agreeing with God's judgements, His verdicts, and His counsel, on any given matter; hating what He hates, and loving what He loves, begins when the soul and spirit within man bows to the will and to the purpose of God.

CHAPTER

Chapter Eight

ACTIVE HOLINESS

Active holiness is a fruit or a by-product of passive holiness. When the temple, or the vessel, is dedicated unto the LORD, it will produce that for which it is purposed. When our lives are dedicated and hallowed unto God, then works of genuine holiness will follow.

It must be made very clear that no personal work that we ever do can possibly make us holy. We cannot purchase holiness by anything that we choose to do. Deeds or works of holiness that are performed apart from our dedication unto God often result as works of legalism.

Works of legalism are works performed for the sake of purchasing or gaining favor with God. They are works that are done in an attempt to create or to gain holiness or righteousness. Works of legalism seek to find merit with God with the idea of transforming a person to a higher level of spiritual status. There is nothing that we could ever do to purchase favor with God or to create true holiness. The way that we live our lives does not produce holiness. The reality is that our lives reflect the true holiness that has been obtained through our faith, persuasion, commitment and dedication unto God. Deeds of holiness are an effect, not the cause.

God does, however, require works and deeds of active holiness. A dedicated temple produces the works for which the temple is dedicated. The true fruit of holiness is moral purity, integrity, sanctification and righteousness. As already stated in this book, *"Being dedicated, set apart and hallowed unto God precedes all moral behavior, or doing."*

For the grace of God that bringeth salvation hath appeared to all men, Teaching us that, denying ungodliness and worldly lusts, we should live soberly, righteously, and godly, in this present world; Looking for that blessed hope, and the glorious appearing of the great God and our Saviour Jesus Christ; Who gave himself for us, that he might redeem us from all iniquity, and purify unto himself a peculiar people, zealous of good works (Titus 2:11-14).

God's Grace not only brought us salvation, but also teaches us to live a clean, sober, righteous and

Godly life before God. Jesus gave Himself not only to redeem us from all iniquity, but also to purify *unto Himself* a peculiar people, zealous of good works.

These verses in Titus sum it all up in reality. Many teach and believe that the work of redemption is only the saving of the soul. Yes, Jesus died to save us. But, He also died to bring us unto holiness. He did so by PURIFYING UNTO HIMSELF A PECULIAR PEOPLE.

The word peculiar in the Aramaic New Testament is *seg-ool-law'* meaning *to shut up; wealth, a jewel, peculiar treasure, proper, good, and special.*

Take a moment to look up the following scriptures concerning God's people being peculiar: Exodus 19:5, Deuteronomy 14:2, Deuteronomy 26:18, Psalm 135:4, Titus 2:14, 1 Peter 2:9.

God has always required, and still requires, that His people be distinctively different. Baruch Levine writes in his book, "Biblical Concepts of Holiness": ...*"that the people of Israel, in becoming a holy nation, must preserve its distinctiveness from other peoples. It must pursue a way of life different from that practiced by other peoples".*

As a peculiar people, it was God's original purpose and intent that Israel be a nation of priests, a holy nation, dedicated unto Him and to His service. God severed His people from all others for this purpose.

And ye shall be holy unto me: for I the LORD am holy, and have severed you from other people, that ye should be mine (Leviticus 20:26).

And ye shall be unto me a kingdom of priests, and an holy nation. These are the words which thou shalt speak unto the children of Israel. (Exodus 19:6).

Imagine, being called by the Almighty to be a nation of priests. What a privilege, what a calling, and what a mandate! The question is however, "What is a priest?" A priest is one who has access to the presence of God. A priest ministers first and foremost unto God, not unto the people.

And I, behold, I have taken your brethren the Levites from among the children of Israel: to you they are given as a gift for the LORD, to do the service of the tabernacle of the congregation. Therefore thou and thy sons with thee shall keep your priest's office for everything of the altar, and within the vail; and ye shall serve: I have given your priest's office unto you as a service of gift: and the stranger that cometh nigh shall be put to death (Numbers 18:6-7)

And the priest shall make an atonement for him before the LORD: *(Leviticus 6:7)*

There are literally multitudes of scriptures that express the work and ministry of the priesthood. The verses that express the various natures of the priest's ministry and the commands of God have one thing in common. Each of these verses clearly states that no matter the ministry or duty of the priest within the tabernacle/temple, their service was always conducted and performed *before the LORD*!

Leviticus 4:6.17 - The blood was sprinkled seven times before the LORD
Leviticus 4:7 - The priest applied blood to the horns of the Golden Altar before the LORD.
Leviticus 6:7 - The priest made atonement before the LORD
Leviticus 14:12 - Wave offerings were made before the LORD
Leviticus 16:30 - Sins were cleansed before the LORD
Numbers 6:16 - The Sin and Burnt offerings were before the LORD

These verses reveal how that everything the priests did was *'before the LORD'.* This is the calling of the priesthood. It is not a ministry first and foremost that is performed before man. Oh yes, man benefits from the ministry of the priest. However, man benefits from the service of the priest due to the LORD's reaction to the ministry of the priest. In other words, as God reacts with His favor and pleasure upon the ministry of the priest serving before His face, the pleasure and presence of God spills over and touches those surrounding the priest. A priest's ministry is only as effective to those around him, as much as is his service and dedication to the LORD.

A priest was dedicated unto God for the purpose of serving God. The priest was to be holy unto the LORD. Only then could he function as a priest and minister in and among the holy things of God and before the presence of the LORD.

Dedication unto God leads to *active duty or doing.* A soldier is sworn into duty prior to being sent into an active battle. In like manner, a priest is dedicated and hallowed into his service before he can successfully function within the office unto which he has been called.

The high priest under the Law of Moses was a picture of our High Priest, Jesus. The high priest was crowned with a golden crown, and engraved on the crown were these words: *HOLINESS TO THE LORD.* Is there any wonder as to why holiness was such a huge aspect for the priesthood?

And they made the plate of the holy crown of pure gold, and wrote upon it a writing, like to the engravings of a signet, HOLINESS TO THE LORD. (Exodus 39:30)

The crown on the high priest's head was not first and foremost a crown of ruling, kingship, authority, or power. It was a witness of a life dedicated and set apart unto an office or calling. The crown on the high priest's head was a crown of holiness!

The word used for *crown* in Hebrew is very significant and powerful. It is the Hebrew word *neh-zer*, and it means something that is set apart, dedication (of a priest or Nazarite); unshorn locks; a chaplet (especially of royalty), consecration, crown, hair, and separation.

The word *Nazarite*, or *Naw-zeer*, and the word *crown*, both come from the same Hebrew root word, *Naw-zar*. *Naw-zar* which means to hold aloof, abstain (from food and drink, from impurity, and even from divine worship) (that is, apostatize), specifically to set apart (to sacred purposes), devote, consecrate, and separate self.

The high priest was consecrated and hallowed unto His service through dedication unto the LORD. His crown of holiness also carried the power of royalty. God's priests were called to be a royal priesthood.

In the New Testament Dispensation God has a called and chosen generation that is set apart as a royal priesthood.   This is a priesthood that is dedicated unto God. This is not accomplished first and foremost by what the chosen generation does. Rather, it is accomplished by who the chosen generation is; or in other words what they *be*. As God said, "BE YE HOLY!" As we 'be', we will also 'do', and always in that order.

The Church of Philadelphia, the Bridal church, was admonished by the Lord Jesus to 'hold that fast which thou hast, that no man take thy crown.' (*Revelation 3:11*) In the Aramaic New Testament, the word crown is also *neh-zer*.

The Lord's admonition should cause a stirring in our spirits. We must hold fast to that which He has given us and not allow anything, any man, any idea, any falsehood, any wind of doctrine or any temptation, to take away the royal crown of holiness unto the Lord. There is a war going on in the spiritual world these days. This battle has been waged by the forces of darkness against God's people with the intent of taking away the crown of *Holiness unto the LORD.* No wonder the Philadelphia Church was admonished to hold fast and not allow the crown to be stolen.

But ye are a chosen generation, a royal priesthood, an holy nation, a peculiar people; that ye should shew forth the praises of him who hath called you out of darkness into his marvellous light: (1 Peter 2:9)

CHOSEN GENERATION means elected stock, offspring, chosen out from, and elected (John 15:16 - I have chosen you.)

ROYAL PRIESTHOOD means kingly priests, having priestly authority (Psalm 110:4 – David was a kingly priest, as well as a prophet.)

HOLY NATION means sacred, pure, dedicated, set apart, consecrated tribe or race. (I Peter 2:9)

PECULIAR PEOPLE means purchased, bought, paid for (different because of to whom you belong)

(Eph. 1:14 / 1 Corinthians 6:19-20 - Ye are bought with a price.)

Being a chosen generation, a royal priesthood, a holy nation and a peculiar people is manifest in the lives of God's elect in that they *SHOW FORTH THE PRAISES OF GOD*. What does it mean to show forth the praises of God? Does it simply mean to go to church and sing, worship, raise your hands, clap and dance? No, definitely not, even though that is part of it. Praise and worship are only a small part of fulfilling this mandate.

Showing forth the praises of God has to do with your actions and deeds demonstrating and revealing the majesty and the power of God! In other words, the life that you live demonstrates His praise. We can all worship on Sunday. However, does the rest of your life reveal who God is?

The total existence of those who were called to the priesthood was to demonstrate and to show forth the praises of God. This was not only seen in their daily service unto the LORD, but was also seen outside of their service. The priests were not only priests while or when they ministered at the altars or elsewhere throughout the temple. The priesthood was a *life calling*; a life that was separated unto God; a life of service unto the

LORD, both within and without of the tabernacle/temple. A priest was a priest continuously. The mantle of the priest did not lift off of the priest when he took off his priestly garments. The calling of the priesthood was continuous, every moment of every day and life-long.

Without father, without mother, without descent, having neither beginning of days, nor end of life; but made like unto the Son of God; abideth a priest continually. (Hebrews 7:3)

Jesus, the Melchizedek High-priest, is a priest continually, without interruption and always. Jesus is the example of the continual state of the priesthood that God's elect is chosen unto.

Many people these days' live dual lives. One moment they are a priest unto God, but the next moment they are serving the flesh and the world. This is not a life of holiness! This is not dedication. A true priest unto God lives the priesthood and in so doing shows forth God's praise.

To *shew forth* means to bring tidings, be a messenger, and to celebrate. The word *praises* means: virtue, excellence, strength, and manliness.

Our lives are to demonstrate, portray, exhibit, and be a messenger of the virtues, excellence and strength of God. This is what Paul meant when he wrote to the Corinthians the following words:

For ye are bought with a price: therefore glorify God in your body, and in your spirit, which are God's. (1 Corinthians 6:20)

Ye are bought with a price; be not ye the servants of men. (1 Corinthians 7:23)

Living a life of devotion means to exhibit who God is through our deeds, actions, and works. By glorifying Him in our bodies and spirits, we show forth the praises of Him who has called us out of darkness and into His marvelous light.

Dedication unto God is lost when our life becomes wrapped up in service to men and not unto God. In serving God we will most certainly serve man. God requires this. However, serving man is not necessarily about serving God, quite the contrary.

For he that is called in the Lord, being a servant, is the Lord's freeman: likewise also he that is called, being free, is Christ's servant. Ye are bought with a price; be not ye the servants of men. Brethren, let every man, wherein he is called, therein abide with God. (1 Corinthians 7:22-24)

Once again, we are given the message of *'ownership'*. We are bought with a price, we are owned. God did not purchase us with His own blood to be bound in service to men. Rather, He purchased us and called us to serve Him by the showing forth of His praises. In doing so, our lives impact, influence, and minister to men. It is an irrevocable principle; a life that is dedicated unto God will touch the lives of men. However, our goal should never be to serve men; it should only and always be to serve God!

Not with eyeservice, as menpleasers; but as the servants of Christ, doing the will of God from the heart; With good will doing service, as to the Lord, and not to men: (Ephesians 6:6-7)

Giving eyeservice means to offer sight-labor. In other words, you do what you do to be seen, heard, and acknowledged by those for whom you perform. God calls this behavior, *'men-pleasers'*. It is not possible to be a man-pleaser and at the same time be dedicated unto God. It is not possible to serve two masters. Outwardly and publicly, some Christians demonstrate great acts of holiness and separation. Unfortunately, in many cases they do so with eyeservice and for the sake of pleasing men. This is not holiness. Rather, this is bondage.

True holiness can only be experienced by sincere commitment, devotion, and dedication unto God. When a life is dedicated unto God, it does not matter what people think or say about you. They may love you or hate you; praise you or revile you; exalt you or humiliate you; accept you or reject you. None of that matters when dedication unto God is the cause and the reason for how you live your life and serve Him. Dedication unto God is possessing a heart that is fixed.

My heart is fixed, O God, my heart is fixed: I will sing and give praise. (Psalm 57:7)

A life dedicated unto God does not seek man's favor. A life dedicated unto God does not desire or request man's recognition. A life dedicated unto God does not attempt to please man. Rather, a life dedicated unto God pursues Him! In so doing, both the flesh and the spirit are enmeshed in glorifying God and showing forth His praises. A fixed heart will sing and give praise no matter the circumstance.

Behold, I am the LORD, the God of all flesh: is there any thing too hard for me? (Jeremiah 32:27)

God is the originator and the creator of all flesh. The word for flesh in Hebrew is *baw-sawr.* It comes from the root word *baw-sar* which means to be fresh, to announce glad news, to be a messenger, preach, publish, shew forth, and to bear, bring, carry, preach, and tell good tidings.

We all have flesh. The flesh is called the body. Our body has a greater purpose than to simply house our soul and spirit. Our body has a greater purpose than that of strutting through life in an attempt to draw the eyes of man to "self". Our body is the ultimate messenger! Everything that we do with our bodies is exhibiting and proclaiming a message.*

A vessel that is dedicated unto God will proclaim God, and not self. True dedication will announce and publish the holiness of a holy God. Our body is continuously preaching without words. To whomever or to whatever you are dedicated unto will be revealed in your preaching. Your body has language and it screams more loudly than you realize.

(*Dressing to Please The Lord – by Paul M Hanssen – available on amazon.com in Kindle and paperback)

And the very God of peace sanctify you wholly; and I pray God your whole spirit and soul and body be preserved blameless unto the coming of our Lord Jesus Christ. Faithful is he that calleth you, who also will do it. (1 Thessalonians 5:23-24)

For this is the will of God, even your sanctification, that ye should abstain from fornication: That every one of you should know how to possess his vessel (his body) in sanctification and honour (1 Thessalonians 4:3-4)

I beseech you therefore, brethren, by the mercies of God, that ye present your bodies a living sacrifice, holy, acceptable unto God, which is your reasonable service. (Romans 12:1)

What? know ye not that your body is the temple of the Holy Ghost which is in you, which ye have of God, and ye are not your own? For ye are bought with a price: therefore glorify God in your body, and in your spirit, which are God's. (1 Corinthians 6:19-20)

All of the above verses lay emphasis on active, external deeds, and expressions of holiness. God requires active holiness. Active holiness is visible. Active holiness is loud. Active holiness displays the passive commitment and devotion of the heart.

Active holiness seeks to please God.

But now being made free from sin, and become servants to God, ye have your fruit unto holiness, and the end everlasting life. (Romans 6:22)

The fruit of redemption is holiness. The manifestation of servanthood unto God is holiness. To be a servant means to be dedicated unto a master. God, the Master, requires that our bodies be treated as His temple, the place where He resides. He demands that our bodies be messengers that show forth His praise, His excellency, and His power. Are you part of the chosen generation? If so, shew forth His praises!

CHAPTER

Chapter Nine

THE EFFECT
OF HOLINESS

The effects of true holiness in the life of a dedicated believer are manifold. The following examples give us a glimpse into some of the effects and the rewards of holiness.

A) To See God

Surely, it must be clear to the reader that God is tremendously serious about holiness. As a matter of fact, it is such a serious matter that God promises that without holiness no man will see Him. Holiness opens the eyes of the spirit within the heart of man to see God.

Follow peace with all men, and holiness, without which no man shall see the Lord: (Hebrews 12:14)

Many would say that this verse has to do with the end of time when mankind stands before the judgement throne of God. This cannot be true because all of the dead and the living, not just the holy, will stand before the Creator. All of mankind will stand before God and give an account of him/herself before Him. All will see Him, all tongues will confess Him, and all knees will bow before Him.

Therefore, I do not believe that this verse is speaking of seeing God in the future, but rather seeing Him in 'the now'. Defilement and impurity are the cause of spiritual blindness. Purity, however, opens the inner eyes of the spirit to see that which is of the spirit.

Blessed are the pure in heart: for they shall see God. (Matthew 5:8)

When the heart is dedicated and purified unto God, the pollutions which hinder the view of Him are removed. Pollution of mind and spirit obstruct spiritual vision. In contrast, purity clears the sight.

I recall visiting a large city within a country where I had been sent to minister. One of the memorable features of this city was a large beautiful mountain that was an impressive backdrop to the hustle and bustle of daily life. I had seen pictures of the mountain before arriving and I was impressed by the mountain's size, beauty, and proximity to the city. One day, as we drove about, I asked my host,

"Where is that beautiful mountain that everyone talks about?" To my shocking surprise my host said, "It is right over there to your left." I thought that he was joking because I saw nothing but smog, haze, and a mist. "Believe me", he said, "It is there."

The mountain, as large as it was, was out of view. It was hidden behind a curtain of gray pollution that had been generated by the inhabitants of the city. This reminded me of mankind's inability to see God due to the pollutions generated within his own heart.

True holiness opens spiritual eyes to see God in all things! If you are unable to see clearly into your personal spiritual world (and beyond), the first place of examination should be the impurities that are lurking within the heart and mind.

B) Power

True holiness and devotion activate the power of God to work in the life of the believer. In like manner, God's power actively working in the believer's life produces holiness. Hence, holiness produces power and His power produces holiness. This principle of truth works both ways.

And declared to be the Son of God with power,

according to the spirit of holiness, by the resurrection from the dead: (Romans 1:4)

Jesus was holiness personified. He was totally dedicated and devoted unto His Father's will. Hence, He lived His life, accomplished His deeds, and acted out His calling in absolute holiness. There was no sin found in Him. He was separate from sinners and undefiled.

For such an high priest became us, who is holy, harmless, undefiled, separate from sinners, and made higher than the heavens; (Hebrews 7:26)

Death could not hold His body, because His body was holy. Death could not decay His body, because He was holy. Holiness produces a power over death and over spirits of death. The dark and evil side of the spirit world flees from the power of holiness. The presence and glory of holiness is earth shaking and life giving.

Holiness carries a powerful presence. Demons tremble in the presence of holiness. Victory breaks forth in the powerful presence of holiness. Holiness is the glory and majesty of God revealed.

Who is like unto thee, O LORD, among the gods? who is like thee, glorious in holiness, fearful in praises, doing wonders? (Exodus 15:11)

Oh, I love this verse! Who is like the LORD? Among all of the gods of this world, there is none like Him. He is glorious in holiness. His holy presence is great and magnificent. His holy presence invokes fearful praises. This simply means that His magnificent holiness demands honor, reverence, and respect. His holy presence performs wonders. There is nothing like the holiness of God. It is full of power, life, majesty, and might.

When God was about to reveal His power in the defeat of Jericho, Joshua commanded the people to sanctify themselves.

And Joshua said unto the people, Sanctify yourselves: for tomorrow the LORD will do wonders among you. (Joshua 3:5)

Through Joshua, God was basically saying, "I will reveal my power through a sanctified, holy people."

Repentance, sanctification and holiness manifest the power of God that produces revival. On the other hand, revival ushers in the spirit of repentance and sanctification that leads unto holiness. It is evident that this principle works either way. God will do wonders among a people that are dedicated to Him. In like manner, His wonders will produce devotion and dedication unto Him.

C) Joy and Happiness

Man's hunger for joy and happiness is evidenced in almost every aspect of society. We eat to be happy. We go on vacation seeking for thrills and happiness. We get married because we are looking for happiness. We have a family because we are looking for the ultimate happiness. We seek all manner of entertainment because we are searching for the thrill of happiness. We seek the gain of material things in the hopes of filling a void with happiness. Our lives revolve around the desperate attempt of finding joy and happiness. However, there is only one thing that will ever grant us the fulfillment of that which we seek after. God is the only answer to this search.

True satisfaction and joy are experienced when God, Himself, is satisfied and when He is *'joyed'*. *God satisfied is man satisfied*! Separating one's life unto God produces true joy. Holiness is, therefore, happiness!

Blessed is the man that walketh not in the counsel

of the ungodly, nor standeth in the way of sinners, nor sitteth in the seat of the scornful. But his delight is in the law of the LORD; and in his law doth he meditate day and night. And he shall be like a tree planted by the rivers of water, that bringeth forth his fruit in his season; his leaf also shall not wither; and whatsoever he doeth shall prosper (Psalm 1:1-3).

The word blessed in Hebrew is *eh'-sher*. This word means happiness. Blessedness is therefore happiness. Happy is the man who walks a separated, holy life, set apart from the ungodly, sinners, and the scornful. Those who delight in God's Law and mediate therein day and night will find stability and fruitfulness in life. It is a sad reality that man spends his life spinning his wheels looking for happiness and yet, he rejects the source that provides it.

C. S. Lewis wrote the following words to an American friend of his, "How little people know who think that holiness is dull. When one meets the real thing, it is irresistible. If even ten percent of the world's population had it, would not the whole world be converted and happy before a year's end?"

Powerful words! True happiness is found in holiness unto the LORD!

Obviously, much, much more could be written on the subject of dedication, devotion and holiness unto the LORD. However, I trust that the words in this book, even though incomplete, will assist you in having a better understanding of this powerful topic and life changing principle of holiness at work in your life.

But as he which hath called you is holy, so be ye holy in all manner of conversation; Because it is written, Be ye holy; for I am holy. (1 Peter 1:15-16)

The End

<u>PERSONAL NOTES</u>

PERSONAL NOTES

PERSONAL NOTES

PERSONAL NOTES